Grace: It's Not What You Think

Steven Waldron

Copyright 2022 by Steven Waldron.

Published 2022.

Printed in the United States of America.

All rights reserved.

No portion of this book may be reproduced, stored in a retrieval system, or transmitted in any form or by any means – electronic, mechanical, photocopy, recording, scanning, or other – except for brief quotations in critical reviews or articles, without the prior written permission of the author.

ISBN 978-1-950647-98-9

Cover image: CanStockPhoto 7201115

Publishing assistance by BookCrafters, Parker, Colorado.
www.bookcrafters.net

Introduction

IN WRITING THIS BOOK, I have to say I am indebted to my Instructors at Jackson College of Ministries. They seem to have had a right consensus on Biblical grace, and taught the students accordingly. Among these fabulous Instructors were Gordon Mallory, Sidney Poe, Ruby Martin, David Bernard, David Reever, Darrell Johns, Alan Oggs (a truly great man), Thomas Craft, Jonathon Urshan, Elton and Loretta Bernard, and Floyd Odom, among others. As a Staff, they exemplified grace as well as taught it. I am forever indebted and grateful for their faithfulness to the grace of God.

Chapter 1

GRACE IS A BEAUTIFUL WORD. There are few words that are spoken that are as pleasant as grace. Love can be misunderstood. There are different kinds of love. The Greeks knew of at least four. But when grace hits the ear, as it rolls off a tongue, instantly, the atmosphere is lifted. There is a joyous buoyancy, even if ever so slight. Grace is when we do get what we don't deserve. It is unmerited favor. Mercy, on the other hand, is when we don't get what we do deserve. It could be said that the theme of the Bible is grace. God graciously gave a beautiful, sinless, bountiful world, full of life and vigor, based solely on His grace. He made Adam and Eve in His Image, and placed them in that world, solely predicated on His grace. And after mankind in rebellion sinned, God provided a way of salvation for all men, based uniquely on His grace.

Even Heaven and the various classes of beings in the supernatural world were created by God's grace. The current material world, though darkened by sin, still pulsates with God's grace.

Unfortunately, with such unmerited favor abounding, some have attempted to take advantage of grace. They have misinterpreted what Biblical grace is and what it means. Grace, as we shall see, is the opportunity to be free from sin and live for God. That is true beauty and liberty. Grace is not the ability to sin without ramification. Grace is free but not cheap. Grace is when Holy God did not, and does not, destroy people when they sin, at least immediately, usually. Grace is God's gracious plan of salvation made available to us. Mankind is constantly trying to push the boundaries of God's grace. Rather than seeing it as an opportunity for holiness and relationship, we want it to be about encroachment with the world. How much can I get away with and still be saved?

"Grace, grace, God's grace, Grace that will pardon and cleanse within; Grace, grace, God's grace, Grace that is greater than all our sin!" So goes that 1910 Hymn written by Julia H. Johnston. When I was a young Christian, we sang it often. While the lyrics of this beautiful song are certainly true, grace is beyond this. Let's look at an oft overlooked Scripture detailing God's grace. It is written by Paul to Titus, and says, *"For the grace of God that bringeth salvation hath appeared to all men, Teaching us that, denying ungodliness and worldly lusts, we should live soberly, righteously, and godly, in this present world;"* Titus 2:11, 12.

In Verse 11, we see that salvational grace has appeared to all. How this has happened is a matter of discussion. Some feel Jesus appeared in His resurrected form to all people groups around the world. Some feel this Verse means salvation is available to all. Others think the interpretation is the Gospel was preached in all the world at that point, and there is New Testament evidence to buttress that claim. Still others think this is speaking of Natural Law in Conscience as in Romans 1. Other views could be held also. We could debate the points. But the issue that concerns us at the moment is found in Verse 12. The grace of God that has appeared to all men in Verse 11 teaches us things. Grace teaches us to deny ungodliness and worldly lust. It also teaches us that we should live soberly, righteously, and godly in this present world. This certainly doesn't sound like sin and God doesn't care. But there are other Scriptures as well about grace that counter the easy believe, greasy grace, sloppy agape paradigm, as well.

Before we get into those Scriptures, some may ask, do people actually feel you can sin and still please God? The answer unfortunately, is yes. A prominent denominational Pastor, Author, and Radio Personality was famous for his pronouncement that a saved person committing adultery when Jesus came, in the very bed, would still go to Heaven. This is not an isolated viewpoint. This is certainly not taught in Scripture. How do they arrive at such a conclusion?

Basically it goes like this. Since salvation is dependent upon Jesus, and not us, then losing our salvation is not dependent upon us, either. Since it is all of grace, and Jesus forgives us from all sins past, present, and future, at salvation, it is impossible to be lost once saved. We are not stronger than Jesus. We can't break the covenant even if we try. That is the major argument for most with sloppy agape. Of course, tomes are written elucidating the doctrine, with various nuances of thought, and various Scriptures brought in. But that is the basic gist. And not everyone that believes that sin and moral failure is alright with God believe in the perseverance of the saints, or once saved always saved. They key is not our thoughts, however. But what say the Scriptures?

Romans 6:1 and 2 read: *"What shall we say then? Shall we continue in sin, that grace may abound?"*

"God forbid. How shall we, that are dead to sin, live any longer therein?" Again, this doesn't sound like God approves of sin at all. Grace is not the unmerited position of God overlooking our sin. Rather, it is the unmerited favor of God to give us an opportunity to be saved, when we should be destroyed. Grace is the plan of salvation. It is God wooing us, and drawing us, without us asking. It is He coming to shed His blood for us in atonement, not because we are good, but because He is good. Grace may have a component of God not immediately killing us and sending us to hell when we sin once, as well. But in Verse 1, Paul asks, should we continue in sin that grace may abound? Verse 2 gives the emphatic answer, God forbid. So grace is not an excuse to sin. Paul wanted to expose in Romans a false teaching that he had been accused of. It went something like this: If sin shows God's grace, shouldn't we sin more, so God's grace should abound? Paul eviscerates this doctrine and accusation in Romans. Paul's conclusion of this false teaching is summed up in Romans 3:8 which reads, *"And not rather, (as we be slanderously reported, and as some affirm that we say,) Let us do evil, that good may come? whose damnation is just."* The Context is Verses 5-7 of Chapter 3. Here we see grace has been falsely represented for quite some time, even in Paul's day. Verses 5-7 read thusly, *"But if our unrighteousness commend the righteousness of God, what shall we say? Is God unrighteous who taketh vengeance? (I speak as a man) God forbid: for then how shall God judge the world? For if the truth of God hath more abounded through my lie unto his glory; why yet am I also judged as a sinner?"* Grace has to do with God's love and mercy. It is no invitation for the Christian to sin.

Chapter 2

WHAT IS THE INTERACTION BETWEEN GRACE AND WORKS? Do works play any role at all with grace? The answer is no. But with that being said, we must understand that God's grace is multi-sided, as alluded to in Chapter 1. What do I mean by "multi-sided"?

In the first most basic aspect of grace, it is God's unmerited favor. I realize this definition has fallen out of favor with many of late. But it is really a good summation in one phrase of the meaning of "charis," or grace in Greek. So God, with no consultation with anyone, decided before the foundation of the world to save a people He knew would fall based on His Omniscient foreknowledge. Also in this foreknowledge, He knew who would receive His grace and who would of their own free will reject it. Foreknowledge is not causative, or else free will is not free will. For man to have a real choice, he had to have freedom of will. We may explore that later. Where grace comes in with the subject at hand is the fact that God created this plan before the foundation of the world, where He would come in flesh (sent His Son), and die for mankind. He then would elevate saved mankind to be His sons and daughters throughout eternity, seeing Him, and actually being like Him. This is the essence of preemptive grace. Now it goes deeper than this.

Some of these concepts we have already dealt with, at least superficially in Chapter 1. God not only has this great plan. He preemptively, predicated solely on his amazing love and grace, decides to pour out His Spirit on all flesh. He also decides that He would draw all men unto Himself. And that He would be the True Light, lighting every man that comes into the world. And that man, in all of our rebellion and sin, could have faith sparked by hearing the Word of God (Romans 10:17). That satan would not be powerful enough to stop us from responding. This is all born of grace. We have nothing at all to do with any of this.

Then grace would have a plan of salvation that was powerful enough for us to live for God. We could overcome the world, the flesh, and the devil. Grace would allow us to share the Faith with others. Grace would give us power over the enemy, and endue us with gifts and fruit. Grace enables us to pray effectually. And grace gives us an eternity in Heaven with Jesus in a glorified body. So, grace is multi-faceted. We have nothing to do with God implementing any of this in His redemptive plan. When we sin, we have an advocate with the Father. Why? Because of grace. That is the way God in His Sovereignty decreed it. It is perfect. Because God did it. It is all of grace. Grace is a gift. He preemptively and sovereignly did each of these things. And still, it nowhere indicates predestination over freewill, or an allowance of sin with no repercussions.

Predestination is the destination, so to speak. It is not God superimposing His will on us to make us be saved even when we do not want to be. Rather, it is in His sovereign plan that the whosoever will be saved, will be filled with the Holy Ghost, will be baptized in His Name. God predestinates certain things to people making certain decisions, not predestinating them to make the decisions.

Regarding sin, sin has to be dealt with. God is holy, so sin cannot dwell in His presence, or with Him for eternity. And Jesus' Blood is the cure for sin. 1 John 1:7 gives a key to walking sinless in grace. It says, "But if we walk in the light, as he is in the light, we have fellowship one with another, and the blood of Jesus Christ his Son cleanseth us from all sin." Notice "but if" that begins this Verse. This is a contingent clause. This means the subject of the Verse is contingent on fulfilling certain criteria. So to continue in the Verse, our criteria is to walk in the light as he is in the light. Not in light, mind you. But walking in the light as he is in the light. It is a specific light as indicated by the modifier "the" before light. If we do this, we have fellowship one with another, and the blood of Jesus Christ cleanseth us from all sin. Notice, the blood is not a one-time application. It is a continual cleansing. It has an initial application, but continues to cleanse predicated on our walking in the light. As stated earlier, sin must be dealt with. Jesus carried our sins in a substitutionary fashion at Calvary. The sin problem was dealt with there. But it is only applied to our life by obeying the Gospel. And it remains effectual in our life by walking in His light. So, grace is the opportunity, not the unconditional force of overriding freewill. It is multi-sided, but with one overarching vision. God has sovereignly chosen the means and results of choosing grace, and all of the various associated nuances.

Chapter 3

Let's look at how grace is played out in various lives and situations in the Bible. First, we will look at Abraham. We may not look at each in chronological order, or in order of significance. But each will be valuable in understanding the true Biblical meaning of grace, away from the somewhat perverted false view that is manifested in so much of Christendom. Let's begin.

Abram, as his pre-covenant name was called, was sovereignly chosen by God to be in the lineage of the Messiah. While his family was in Ur worshipping other gods (Joshua 24:2,3), God called him to go to a land he did not know and look for a city he had never seen (Hebrews 11:8-10). God, by His grace kept him from death, kept Sarai with him in Egypt, and gave him promises of land and seed. This is all of grace. *"Abraham believed God, and it was accounted unto him for righteousness"* (Genesis 15:6; Romans 4:3; Galatians 3:6; James 2:23). Yet the precursor to believing God, the evidence, is found in James 2:20-22. It reads:

"But wilt thou know, O vain man, that faith without works is dead?"

"Was not Abraham our father justified by works, when he had offered Isaac his son upon the altar?"

"Seest thou how faith wrought with his works, and by works was faith made perfect?"

Then Verse 23 says, *"And the scripture was fulfilled which saith, Abraham believed God, and it was imputed unto him for righteousness: and he was called the Friend of God."*

So, Abraham had grace mixed with works. God did so much for him by grace. Grace was the opportunity, the promises, provision, and protection. But Abram in Ur doesn't receive the promises. He has to travel to the Promised Land. Abraham without offering Isaac doesn't obtain the promises. So grace, God's sovereign grace is involved, yes. But Abraham had to believe and act on the opportunity as well. Actions clearly were involved.

Next we come to Noah. Noah was shown grace in the eyes of the LORD (Genesis 6:8). But grace alone did not save Noah from the Flood. Yes, God's grace protected Noah from his wicked and perverse generation. Grace gave him three sons, a wife, and three son's wives willing to go with him into the ark. Grace brought the animals to Noah. Grace gave Noah the plans for the ark. Grace gave Noah the means to build the ark. And so much more. But Noah still had to apply grace. He had to work. He preached. He built. He labored. Noah could not have done it without God's grace. But God's grace alone, without Noah's faith and work would have been meaningless.

Now may be a good time to compare God's grace in the gift of salvation with the reality that occurs. Grace says God nailed every sin for every person to the cross. Grace is God pouring out His Spirit on all flesh. Grace is God drawing every man unto Himself. Grace is the opportunity. Yet the Bible is clear, most people go to hell. *"Strait is the gate, and narrow is the way that leads to eternal life, and few there be that find it."* There are few saved. Jesus said many would seek to enter therein, and not be able (Luke 13:23-24). Faith without works is dead, being alone (James 2:18-26). If you love Jesus, keep His commandments (John 14:15; 15:10). So, grace does not include predestination of the individual or a condoning of sin.

A word may be in order here about predestination, as well. God predestinates the destination, and not the individual. Those who accept the whosever will obtain certain promises. And it is for each individual. But God does not predestinate exclusively with no choice involved by the individual for that destination. God knows but does not choose to the exclusion of others.

Paul is yet another great example of grace, and one some use to promote predestination. Paul, then called Saul, was immersed in

God's grace to see Stephen, and not to be struck dead by God for approving of his stoning. God's grace upon Saul with his Damascus Road experience. Grace allowed Ananias to come and share the Gospel with him. Grace restored his eyesight. But it was Paul's freewill that allowed him to choose to serve Jesus. Grace afforded Paul the enormous opportunity, but Paul chose.

From these few examples, we can see the following: Grace provides the opportunity. Grace does not mean one can sin with no consequences. And grace does not mean we are chosen to serve God regardless of our will.

Chapter 4

I feel a few more examples from the Bible are in order about grace, and what it is. We'll begin with David. David, by God's grace, was chosen King of Israel and anointed. But still, it was because God had sought Him a man after His own heart. David chose to serve God, so God chose him. Grace preserved David when he deserved to die. Grace put David back on the Throne when he had vacated it to Absalom. Grace gave David and Bathsheba another child to serve as Monarch after him. Grace gave David's son Solomon a reign of unprecedented peace and prosperity.

I need to mention here the immersive grace of God. We have just been examining a few mountain peaks of God's grace in the lives of individuals in Scripture. But actually, we are all immersed in grace. Let me explain. There is the grace of life. The fact that we have been chosen to exist, with no consultation in the matter. The grace of thought and consciousness. We can think, feel, and respond. The grace of current living. The grace of beauty, that creation is beautiful, and we can partake in it. The grace of physical attributes. Whatever your state, it could usually be worse, most times, much worse. So, our lives are immersed in grace.

Getting back to individual examples of grace found in Scripture, Peter is an example, or multiple examples of the grace of God. Peter can curse and blaspheme that he does not know Jesus. Yet, he obtained the keys to the Kingdom by knowing who Jesus was by revelation of the Father. Yet, God allowed him to preach the Day of Pentecost message a few weeks after thrice denying that he knew Jesus. Peter was called "satan" by Jesus. But he still walked on water. Peter cut off a man's ear. But Jesus reattached the ear, possibly saving Peter from arrest. Satan wanted to sift Peter as wheat, but Jesus prayed for him. James was beheaded, Peter was delivered. Peter was rebuked by Paul, yet remained an Apostle of the Jews. Peter, as we all are, was a walking testimony of grace.

Jesus' half-brothers were fascinating examples of the grace of God. They mocked Jesus. Yet Jesus when He arose gave orders to tell His brethren that He was risen. In the Old Testament, she bears ripped children who mocked Elisha. But Jesus' brethren were shown grace.

Chapter 5

THE SONG GOES, "Grace, grace, God's grace. Grace that will pardon and cleanse within. Grace, grace, God's grace. Grace, that is greater than all our sin." That is Gloria Gaither's song "Grace Greater Than Our Sin." "Amazing Grace" by John Newton could be called the Hymn of the English language. Who could forget "Jesus Paid It All," or "At the Cross?" "The Old Rugged Cross," "To God be the Glory"? All songs about grace. John and Charles Wesley seemed to understand the grace of God. "O, for a Thousand Tongues to Sing," "Jesus, Lover of My Soul," "Love Divine, All Loves Excelling" are among the 6,500 or so hymns Charles Wesley penned. There is something intrinsic when we hear about the grace of God. It is universal. When we hear about it, it strikes a chord in our soul.

I recall watching Schindler's List several years ago. I don't normally watch Hollywood movies, but this was presented as something like an informative documentary from history. In watching, I remember being moved by the acts of grace perpetrated by certain ones in the film, trying desperately to save the Jews. Grace, when we get what we don't deserve or expect, is seen as a commendable attribute in human nature. Not cheap grace or sloppy agape. Not acts of perfidy hiding behind grace. Not a "do as thou wilt" attitude. But when someone gets unexpected help in a time of distress. This is what God has done for us.

The great love story of the Bible is grace. Mankind getting what God's love gives us, and not what we deserve. Satan and the demons didn't have this extended to them. And God is certainly right in doing this, since whatever He does is right. But Ephesians 2 explains that in the ages to come, we will be certain trophies of grace. We went from the guttermost to the uttermost. Like Esther, we went from orphans to the Throne. Like Joseph, from the pit to the palace. All because He who has all riches became poor for our sake.

The study of the two simple words, "for us" is amazing in Scripture. These two words, in the context of God in Christ, is the essence of grace.

Romans 5:8 reads, *"But God commendeth his love toward us, in that, while we were yet sinners, Christ died for us."*

Romans 8:26 *"Likewise the Spirit also helpeth our infirmities: for we know not what we should pray for as we ought: but the Spirit itself maketh intercession for us with groanings which cannot be uttered."*

Romans 8:31 *"What shall we then say to these things? If God be for us, who can be against us?"*

Romans 8:32 *"He that spared not his own Son, but delivered him up for us all, how shall he not with him also freely give us all things?"*

1 Corinthians 5:7 *"Purge out therefore the old leaven, that ye may be a new lump, as ye are unleavened. For even Christ our passover is sacrificed for us:"*

2 Corinthians 5:21 *"For he hath made him to be sin for us, who knew no sin; that we might be made the righteousness of God in him."*

Galatians 3:13 *"Christ hath redeemed us from the curse of the law, being made a curse for us: for it is written, Cursed is every one that hangeth on a tree:"*

Ephesians 5:2 *"And walk in love, as Christ also hath loved us, and hath given himself for us an offering and a sacrifice to God for a sweetsmelling savour."*

1 Thessalonians 2:10 *"Who died for us, that, whether we wake or sleep, we should live together with him."*

Titus 2:14 *"Who gave himself for us, that he might redeem us from all iniquity, and purify unto himself a peculiar people, zealous of good works."*

Hebrews 6:20 *"Whither the forerunner is for us entered, even Jesus, made an high priest for ever after the order of Melchisedec."*

Hebrews 9:12 *"Neither by the blood of goats and calves, but by his own blood he entered in once into the holy place, having obtained eternal redemption for us."*

Hebrews 9:24 *"For Christ is not entered into the holy places made with hands, which are the figures of the true; but into heaven itself, now to appear in the presence of God for us:"*

Hebrews 10:20 *"By a new and living way, which he hath consecrated for us, through the veil, that is to say, his flesh;"*

Hebrews 11:40 *"God having provided some better thing for us, that they without us should not be made perfect."*

1 Peter 2:21 *"For even hereunto were ye called: because Christ also suffered for us, leaving us an example, that ye should follow his steps:"*

1 Peter 4:1 *"Forasmuch then as Christ hath suffered for us in the flesh, arm yourselves likewise with the same mind: for he that hath suffered in the flesh hath ceased from sin;"*

1 John 3:16 *"Hereby perceive we the love of God, because he laid down his life for us: and we ought to lay down our lives for the brethren."*

All of the above Scriptures show the grace of God Jesus has for us. Whatever He did, He did it for us, that we may be redeemed from all ungodliness. Everything Jesus did, it was substitutionary. It was vicarious. He did it sovereignly out of His good pleasure and will.

The term "sovereign" and its connected terms is many times shied away from in non-Calvinist circles. It has been so misused as to fall into disuse. Yet, nothing else really serves as an adequate term to describe the autonomy of God. He chooses. He makes decrees, another term hidden away so often in freewill assemblages, again for the same reason. But the bondage of the will is not necessitated by these terms. God chooses, He declares, He decrees things because He is sovereign. The fact that He expressly chose to come as Man to save us, chose to suffer and die while shedding His Blood, does not in any way diminish our freewill to choose these things. He planned for us to be sons and daughters of His, He chose it to be so. Yet the individual can reject the invitation.

Predestination has at least one appealing aspect to it. By predestination, I mean the classical Calvinistic doctrine. Total depravity. It totally incapacitates sinful man. It says man is so sinful, that God has to give him the new birth before he can have light enough to choose God. This sounds great, theologically. Anything that debases man and exalts God should be thought of as good, at least, usually. Yet, this is not what we see from Scripture. Man is drawn, convicted, then either accepts or rejects. God lights every man that comes into the world. He draws all. He is not far from all. Man can choose, or else God is unjust, at least in some ways of thinking. Man is depraved, horrifically sinful. "The heart is deceitful above all things and desperately wicked". Yet, with God's help and grace, we can choose to receive Him. "But as many as received him, to them gave he power to become the sons of God, even to them that believe on his name:"

Chapter 6

LET'S EXAMINE SOME SCRIPTURES ON GRACE. Grace or a derivative is found 170 times in 159 Verses according to Blue Letter Bible. The first time we find it used is Genesis 6:8, which reads, "B*ut Noah found grace in the eyes of the LORD."* Let's look at this.

God just plucked Noah out of the mass of humanity and decided to sovereignly choose him, as Noah was just as sinful and wicked as everyone else. Well, not exactly. Here's what the Scripture says.

"These are the generations of Noah: Noah was a just man and perfect in his generations, and Noah walked with God." Genesis 6:9

Noah was a just man, and he walked with God just like his Great-Grandfather Enoch. Enoch also, by the way, took steps to access the available grace of God, by walking with God. Going back to Noah, it seems that God's grace was in response to Noah's walk. This, of course, is not congruent with God's grace coming to save man. In that case, God sovereignly chose a plan, because we were so wicked and had no hope. But now that the plan is in place, and God sovereignly pulls on the entire world to be saved, it is our freewill and choice to accept His sovereign plan. So grace has contextual aspects. God is the Initiator of grace. But sometimes His offer is predicated on our performance. We get into trouble theologically and doctrinally by always trying to force God's grace into one aspect or another, when in reality, it is multi-faceted. So, Noah walked with God and was just (we won't go into the controversial perfect in his generations part), and because of this he obtained grace. His receiving of God's grace was predicated on his performance. A Scripture in summation showing the different aspects of God's grace is found in 1 Peter 4:10, which reads,

"As every man hath received the gift, even so minister the same one to another, as good stewards of the manifold grace of God." Manifold in this Verse means, "diverse aspects."

Next, we come to just Lot, receiving the manifold grace of God. In Genesis 19:19 we read,

"Behold now, thy servant hath found grace in thy sight, and thou hast magnified thy mercy, which thou hast shewed unto me in saving my life; and I cannot escape to the mountain, lest some evil take me, and I die:"

How did Lot receive this grace? Let us look at the ways. 1 Peter 2:7-9 is where we will begin our examination. Verse 7 (*"And delivered just Lot, vexed with the filthy conversation of the wicked:"*) Verse 8 "(*For that righteous man dwelling among them, in seeing and hearing, vexed his righteous soul from day to day with their unlawful deeds;)*" Verse 9 (*"The Lord knoweth how to deliver the godly out of temptations, and to reserve the unjust unto the day of judgment to be punished"*).

From these three Verses we see first of all that Lot was vexed with the lifestyle (conversation) of the wicked. So, in Verse 7 he is called just. In Verse 8 Lot is referred to as a righteous man. Then he is referred to as a righteous soul. In Verse 9 it is insinuated that he was godly. But as you read the Genesis record, it is difficult to see these positive attributes of Lot.

In Genesis 19:29 we see Abraham's involvement in Lot's deliverance. It reads thusly, *"And it came to pass, when God destroyed the cities of the plain, that God remembered Abraham, and sent Lot out of the midst of the overthrow, when he overthrew the cities in the which Lot dwelt."*

In this Passage it seems that Lot's deliverance didn't have anything to do with Lot being just (but notice the theme of being just with Noah and Lot) or righteous. It seems to be predicated upon Abraham. Maybe it was Abraham's prayers that he prayed for Lot. Abraham certainly had Lot in mind with the six-fold intercession he made for Sodom in Genesis 18. Genesis 19:27, 28 may also have a clue of Abraham's prayers for Lot. It says, *"And Abraham gat up early in the morning to the place where he stood before the LORD:"* Verse 27. *"And he looked toward Sodom and Gomorrah, and toward all the land of the plain, and beheld, and, lo, the smoke of the country went up as the smoke of a furnace"* Verse 28.

So it could very well be that Abraham looked toward Sodom and prayed for Lot and his family on a daily basis. And that his prayers had enough effect on Lot, that he and his family (at least part) escaped Sodom, because Lot was just and righteous.

One could nuance in many directions with the exact economy between Abraham, Lot and his righteousness, and God's grace. But needless to say, Lot realized he had found grace in God's eyes. But he was righteous and just, or he would have suffered the same fate as Sodom and Gomorrah. So he did things to access the grace of God.

That is, of course, unless you believe that somehow Abraham's prayers made Lot just and righteous without any commensurate action on Lot's part. But it is difficult to read 2 Peter 2:7-9 and come to that conclusion. Abraham played a role in God's grace to Lot. Lot's righteousness did, as well. But it was still God's grace that saved his life.

Grace is mentioned 25 times in the Book of Romans. It is seen four times in Romans 11:6 alone. Unable, due to size and time constraints to examine every Verse on grace in Scripture, it is fitting to visit some mentions of grace in Romans.

First, we'll look at Romans 3:24. It says, *"Being justified freely by his grace through the redemption that is in Christ Jesus:"* You'll notice that grace is the availability of salvation. Jesus provides means to access that grace. Jesus freely and sovereignly provides grace to whosoever will.

Next we come to Romans 5:2 where we see much the same thing. It reads *"By whom also we have access by faith into this grace wherein we stand, and rejoice in hope of the glory of God."* Faith is seen as the entrance into grace. Other meanings of grace in these contexts twist the clear meaning of Scripture.

In Romans 5:15 we read, *"But not as the offence, so also is the free gift.*

For if through the offence of one many be dead, much more the grace of God, and the gift by grace, which is by one man, Jesus Christ, hath abounded unto many." In Context, once again we see that the grace of God is God's free gift of salvation on humanity. This is further elucidated in Romans 5:17, *"For if by one man's offence death reigned by one; much more they which receive abundance of grace and of the gift of righteousness shall reign in life by one, Jesus Christ."*

Romans 6:1, 2 discredit the idea that grace allows one to sin freely. It reads, *"What shall we say then? Shall we continue in sin, that grace may abound?" "God forbid. How shall we, that are dead to sin, live any longer therein?"* Grace, as our initial Scripture at the beginning of this study, leads away from sin, not to sin, in the individual believer's life. This is reinforced in Romans 6:14 when it says, *"For sin shall not have dominion over you: for ye are not under the law, but under grace."* This is a direct reference to the fact that sin doesn't rule over us, but we are free from it because of grace. Paul once again buttresses this fact under the inspiration of the Holy Ghost in 6:15, *"What then? shall we sin, because we are not under the law, but under grace? God forbid."*

So, Romans seems to be a primary refuge for some who teach that grace is a means to sin without retribution, or that grace means some are chosen without their choice to salvation, while others are chosen to be lost (there are at least three different types of predestination, varying on their degree of God's involvement with sending people to hell). Scripturally, this is shown not to be the case.

Grace also stands for the sovereignty of God in bestowing particular gifts, strengths and weaknesses to individuals. We find this in Romans 12:6, *"Having then gifts differing according to the grace that is given to us, whether prophecy, let us prophesy according to the proportion of faith;"* For example, if someone is good at playing the organ, they may just be a natural at it. We once had the third or fourth best organ player in the world as our Church organist. He was flown by the World Council of Churches to Australia to play for their Worldwide Conference. A Minister at a large, iconic Church in Boston told him that if he would come and play the organ at his Church on Sundays, people would line up around the block to hear him play. This gifted organist told me his sister grew up in his household taking organ lessons just as he did. She practiced possibly harder than he did. Yet he was just naturally gifted at playing the organ. He said she never became more than a mid-level organ player. Some become professional baseball players while rarely practicing, and possibly living a detrimental lifestyle to their health, smoking, drinking, carousing, and the like. Thousands may have a dream to make it to the majors one day, sacrificing, exercising, practicing, eating healthy, watching films, studying the game, getting extra instruction, etc. Yet they may never make it past American Legion ball. God has just naturally gifted people in certain areas, even people who are not saved. Paul refers to this as grace, which it rightfully is. They did not get to choose, God just sovereignly created them that way.

I have written a separate book on unconditional eternal security. Yet I wanted to give an example of a Scripture on grace which seems to clearly teach against it. It is found in 2 Corinthians 6:1 and reads thus, *"We then, as workers together with him, beseech you also that ye receive not the grace of God in vain."* This seems to clearly indicate that we can receive God's grace, and it can eventually be in vain due to our unbelief or sin.

Fascinatingly enough monetary offerings are seen as a grace in Corinthians 8:9, *"And not that only, but who was also chosen of the churches to travel with us with this grace, which is administered by us to the glory of the same Lord, and declaration of your ready mind:"* The Churches had given money to be shared with the saints in Jerusalem. It is called grace. They freely gave as God moved on their heart.

We notice in the greetings, salutations, and farewells, grace is often mentioned. An example is found in Galatians 1:3 which reads, *"Grace be to you and peace from God the Father, and from our Lord Jesus Christ,"* This was a common greeting and farewell of the time, Grace to you or some corollary. An example of a farewell is seen in Galatians 6:18, *"Brethren, the grace of our Lord Jesus Christ be with your spirit. Amen."*

Chapter 7

Other examples of grace found in Scripture are:

In Genesis 32:5 Jacob sent droves of animals to Esau in an effort to find grace in his sight.

Joseph found grace in Potipher's sight in Genesis 39:4. Man, being in the image of God, is able to show grace like God, at least to the degree our fallen nature can.

Exodus 33-34 is an interesting look at the grace of God. Too many people think, at least functionally, that God in the Old Testament is different than God in the New Testament. This is not true. He is the LORD, He changes not (Malachi 3:6). His moral attributes, and His essential Nature as Spirit does not change or alter. So, this exchange with Moses is an interesting perspective on God's grace. The setting is Israel had just sinned with the golden calf. God was understandably angry, with the grace He had shown Israel in bringing them up out of Egypt now being forgotten. Let's examine the dialogue.

Exodus 33:12 *"And Moses said unto the LORD, See, thou sayest unto me, Bring up this people: and thou hast not let me know whom thou wilt send with me. Yet thou hast said, I know thee by name, and thou hast also found grace in my sight."*

33:13 *"Now therefore, I pray thee, if I have found grace in thy sight, shew me now thy way, that I may know thee, that I may find grace in thy sight: and consider that this nation is thy people."*

Here, Moses is appealing to God's grace. He is saying to God that just as God had spoken to him, showing he had found Divine favor, let that same grace be delivered to Israel. This is known as Moses' intercession for Israel.

33:14 *"And he said, My presence shall go with thee, and I will give thee rest."* We see here that God is going to go with Moses. God's presence will give rest, which is indicative of the Holy Ghost Comforter. Rest is an attribute of the Holy Ghost, God's dealing with man. So, grace and the Spirit of God among man is intertwined.

33:15 *"And he said unto him, If thy presence go not with me, carry us not up hence."*

33:16 *"For wherein shall it be known here that I and thy people have found grace in thy sight? is it not in that thou goest with us? so shall we be separated, I and thy people, from all the people that are upon the face of the earth."*

Notice in Verse 16 God's grace is associated with His Presence, and this Presence separates God's people from other people on the earth. This is clearly a type of Holy Spirit baptism. It resides with God's people today, and is the source of our separation from the world.

33:17" *And the LORD said unto Moses, I will do this thing also that thou hast spoken: for thou hast found grace in my sight, and I know thee by name."*

33:18 *"And he said, I beseech thee, shew me thy glory."*

33:19 *"And he said, I will make all my goodness pass before thee, and I will proclaim the name of the LORD before thee; and will be gracious to whom I will be gracious, and will shew mercy on whom I will shew mercy."* Notice here that the revelation of God's Presence is associated with His grace.

As God passes by and shows Moses His Presence (to what degree, that is a discussion for another time, since no one can see God and live, according to Scripture), God declares His graciousness among His other attributes. 34:6 says, *"And the LORD passed by before him, and proclaimed, The LORD, The LORD God, merciful and gracious, longsuffering, and abundant in goodness and truth,"*

The middle part of the Priestly Blessing of Numbers 6:24-6 is about grace. Verse 25 says, *"The LORD make his face shine upon thee, and be gracious unto thee:"*

Ruth sought for grace (Ruth 2:2, 10). Hannah found grace (1 Samuel 1:18). David sought for God's grace concerning the child he had born with Bathsheba (2 Samuel 12:22). Mephibosheth is, of course, a preeminent recipient of grace found in Scripture. Israel's days were prolonged because of God's grace (2 Kings 13:23).

Some more Passages that are interesting on grace are:

Zechariah 4:7 *"Who art thou, O great mountain? before Zerubbabel thou shalt become a plain: and he shall bring forth the headstone thereof with shoutings, crying, Grace, grace unto it."*

Zechariah 12:10 *"And I will pour upon the house of David, and upon the inhabitants of Jerusalem, the spirit of grace and of supplications: and they shall look upon me whom they have pierced, and they shall mourn for him, as one mourneth for his only son, and shall be in bitterness for him, as one that is in bitterness for his firstborn."*

As we enter the New Testament, more fascinating Scriptures on grace are found. This is by no means a conclusive list.

Speaking of Jesus, Luke 2:40 reads, *"And the child grew, and waxed strong in spirit, filled with wisdom: and the grace of God was upon him."*

Once again, speaking of Jesus we read, *"And all bare him witness, and wondered at the gracious words which proceeded out of his mouth. And they said, Is not this Joseph's son?"* Luke 4:22

Two Scriptures in John 1 again speak of Jesus in connection with grace. John 1:14 *"And the Word was made flesh, and dwelt among us, (and we beheld his glory, the glory as of the only begotten of the Father,) full of grace and truth."* That is so startling in its beauty. Jesus was full of grace.

John 1:17 *"For the law was given by Moses, but grace and truth came by Jesus Christ."* The import of this Passage could scarcely be more profound. Moses gave the Law to the children of Israel. But grace and truth (you'll notice the connection in Verse 14, as well) came by Jesus Christ.

In John 1:16 we see, *"And of his fulness have all we received, and grace for grace."* This speaks of the twofold dimension of God's grace. We live by grace, and we are able to have eternal life because of God's grace in providing it.

The early believers had great grace upon them. Acts 4:33 *"And with great power gave the apostles witness of the resurrection of the Lord Jesus: and great grace was upon them all."*

Barnabas saw the Gentile believers at Antioch, and knew they had been saved by grace. Acts 13:23 *"Who, when he came, and had seen the grace of God, was glad, and exhorted them all, that with purpose of heart they would cleave unto the Lord."*

The Message of Salvation is known as, "the word of his grace" in Acts 14:3, speaking of revival in Iconium. *"Long time therefore abode they speaking boldly in the Lord, which gave testimony unto the word of his grace, and granted signs and wonders to be done by their hands."*

Paul identifies the Gospel as the Gospel of the grace of God. What beauty! *"But none of these things move me, neither count I my life dear unto myself, so that I might finish my course with joy, and the ministry, which I have received of the Lord Jesus, to testify the gospel of the grace of God."* Acts 20:24

Notice the word "grace" was never uttered by Jesus while He was on earth during His earthly incarnation as recorded in Scripture. But since the entire Word of God is His Word, of course, He spake it in Spirit in eternity, and to us today.

The last Verse of Scripture commends to us grace. It reads, *"The grace of our Lord Jesus Christ be with you all. Amen."* Revelation 22:21

Looking over the remaining Scriptures on grace in the Word of God, it is obvious that there are just too many to list now. However, a couple of more will have to suffice, before we examine the use of grace in the Psalms.

"Let the word of Christ dwell in you richly in all wisdom; teaching and admonishing one another in psalms and hymns and spiritual songs, singing with grace in your hearts to the Lord." Colossians 3:16

Colossians 1:6 which says, *"Which is come unto you, as it is in all the world; and bringeth forth fruit, as it doth also in you, since the day ye heard of it, and knew the grace of God in truth:"* This is fascinating, because it means you can know the grace of God in error, meaning you can think you have the grace of God, but be mistaken.

Perhaps a book 2 on Grace will be in order? Perhaps.

Chapter 8

THE USE OF GRACE IN PSALMS is worth a look uniquely its own. Again, due to size constraints, we will have to be selective to a few pertinent Passages on this beautiful subject.

Psalm 45, a beautiful Messianic Psalm, has this to say, *"Thou art fairer than the children of men: grace is poured into thy lips: therefore God hath blessed thee for ever."* Verse 2. Speaking of Messiah in a prophetic sense, grace is poured into His lips. Has anyone ever spake more gracious words than Jesus?

This mighty promise of God is simply stunning in its majesty. It reads, *"For the LORD God is a sun and shield: the LORD will give grace and glory: no good thing will he withhold from them that walk uprightly."* Psalm 84:11 It is difficult to find a more powerful Scripture in Holy Writ. Jehovah Elohim is seen as a sun and a shield. He gives grace and glory. And the unlimited nature of His bountifulness is given to His people. Nothing good will be withheld from those that are holy. This begins now, and will only be fulfilled in a boundless eternity.

Psalm 85:11 describes the merciful aspects of our Holy God. It says, *"But thou, O Lord, art a God full of compassion, and gracious, longsuffering, and plenteous in mercy and truth."* Five different attributes of God are listed here. He is not just compassionate, but He is full of compassion. He defines the word. He is gracious and longsuffering. And He doesn't just possess mercy and truth, He is plenteous or more than enough in these attributes. This certainly correlates to the attributes that God proclaimed before Moses in Exodus 34:6.

Psalm 103:8 states, *"The LORD is merciful and gracious, slow to anger, and plenteous in mercy."* Notice how being gracious is seen with His other attributes of kindness. God is the very definition of grace. Never forget that God is also holy however, and that He sits on the throne of justice. These various attributes of the goodness and severity of God, as explored by Paul are not antithetical, but rather two sides of the same coin. This Davidic Psalm is fitting, as David knew both the immense goodness of God, but also His severity.

Continuing our exploration of grace in Psalms, we come to Psalm 111:4, which reads, *"He hath made his wonderful works to be remembered: the LORD is gracious and full of compassion."* We take note that so often when God's grace or graciousness is mentioned, it is in a context with other attributes so often. God is so immense in His great goodness, multiple words are required to express the various sides or dimensions of it.

Continuing on, in the 112th Psalm, the fourth Verse, we find *"Unto the upright there ariseth light in the darkness: he is gracious, and full of compassion, and righteous."* Another interesting attribute is added to the gracious aspect of God's character: righteousness. God is gracious, yes, but no one should mistake His graciousness as a mono-moral attribute. He is righteous. He will save whom He deems, and the others will be lost. He is righteous in all of His ways and judgments. We are not to question, just to praise, submit, and obey. He may choose to save those that we in our faulty, finite facilities think should be judged. And some may appear so righteous unto men, but God knows the heart.

"Gracious is the LORD, and righteous; yea, our God is merciful." Psalm 116:5. Here, Gracious is the lead virtue mentioned. It is of the LORD's mercies any of us have a chance. He could have rightfully wiped us out. But He has chosen to express His great graciousness to us. Ephesians 2:7 echoes this sentiment, *"That in the ages to come he might*

shew the exceeding riches of his grace in his kindness toward us through Christ Jesus."

Here are two words we don't often put together, but feel they are at odds one with another. Let's look at the Verse, then I'll explain. *"Remove from me the way of lying: and grant me thy law graciously."* Psalm 119:29. Gracious and law are thought to be set against one another. They are not. We can only be saved by Jesus Christ, Who is the fulfillment of the law. After salvation, the power of the Holy Ghost empowers us to live in accordance with God's Holy Law. His Word. If we did not have His law, we would not know how to please Him. So we need His law, hidden in our heart, etched in His Word, to know how to please God. So, God by His grace grants to us the knowledge of His law, how to please Him.

"The LORD is gracious, and full of compassion; slow to anger, and of great mercy." Psalm 145:8. Variations of this range of God's moral goodness (He has no moral badness, whatever He does is right and good by definition.) are found repeatedly in Scripture, and especially here in Psalms. We find once again that Jehovah is gracious (a derivative of grace), leading the other attributes in this Verse.

The definition of a Psalm has been rather elusive. Some equate Psalm with song. Others say it is poetry. After Psalm 73, it says the prayers of David are ended. Psalms are merely the heart cry of communication with God. Psalms delve into the pathos and honesty between creature and Creator. While, of course, they are theological and true, they are emotional. The height of praise and joy, the depth of sorrow, remorse and forgiveness, the contemplativeness of a Psalm 23, the cry of victory, the anguish of defeat and failure. This is Psalms. Some are musical. Some are instructive. Some are of death. Some are of Heaven. Tears bottled, forever rejoicing. Some are prayers. All are creation laid bare, the Creator writ large. And so often they speak of grace.

Chapter 9

The influence of Grace on music, literature and culture. I remember a scene in Schindler's List (I normally don't watch Hollywood movies. This was more of a documentary on one of the greatest tragedies of modern times. Forgive me if you don't think of it as documentary. We will have to agree to disagree. I certainly don't recommend the waste of time on most Hollywood drivel, with its incumbent anti-Biblical morality) where Oskar Schindler is trying to convince a sadistic Nazi death camp commander of the virtue of grace. This commander would take a rifle, and shoot unsuspecting victims from his office window, located several feet above the ground. Schindler saw the barbarity of the massacre, and the random nature of this vile act, performed totally at the commander's will, day by day. Schindler tries to convince the monster of the power of grace. That there was actually more power in grace than in shooting defenseless people. It is a powerful scene. And the commander seems to momentarily get it, due to the tremendous humanitarian presentation of Schindler. But the animal nature of man takes back over, and the image of the Divine in man is once again subsumed.

People often know grace is a virtue. Turning the other cheek, not when you are weak, but when you could destroy the other person, shows strength. I had a friend who showed great grace. He was a Naval Academy graduate. He was a Pastor. A woman began coming to his Church, the Church which he Pastored (more accurately, the other is just a colloquialism). The husband was infuriated at this turn of events. After Church one day, the man met the Pastor on the porch of the Church building. He began to strike the Pastor with a closed fist. With each blow, this Naval Graduate, who knew in his own strength he could kill the man, just kept repeating the phrase, "I love you," "I love you" after each blow. After several blows, the man broke down crying, saying why didn't you fight back? He knew he had experienced grace. That story was shared by the Pastor some three decades or so ago. I don't remember if the man got saved or not. But he had experienced grace, at least on a human level.

Another unique friend of mine was backslidden. He was shot 11 times during a gang initiation ritual. He survived and became a preacher. That's grace. But he also showed grace. Being a paraplegic, he carried a firearm for protection. As he went to get into his truck alone, a thief came up thinking he had an easy prey. The preacher went for his gun, then decided he was ready for Heaven, while his assailant was not. As the perpetrator came upon him, he grabbed him by the wrist and began to plead with him about the love of Jesus. Something happened because the would-be assailant turned and left! What began as a handicapped individual about to rightfully defend himself, probably leading to a sinner entering eternity without God, ended up with grace. The assailant heard a Gospel message, and survived to consider it. Grace.

Yet a third example of grace is with my wife's cousin. They grew up very close. As a bank teller, once she had a robber come in, hand her a note, demanding all of her money. He had a gun. She began to plead with him, that he was created for better than this. That God loved him, and did not want him to go down this path. He listened to her entreaty, hung his head, put his firearm away, and left the bank. He probably would have faced 20 years in prison for armed bank robbery, but grace gave him another chance. In all three examples, it took courage to share grace.

Some of the most popular books and songs of all time involve grace. "Amazing Grace" may be one of the most popular songs of all time. It was written by a former slave ship captain, who had himself been captured and enslaved, who came to the LORD, and was disgusted with his sin of transporting slaves. "Amazing grace, how sweet the sound, who saved a wretch like me. I once was lost, but now am found, was blind, but now I see. 'Twas grace that taught my heart to fear, and grace my fears relieved; How precious did that grace appear, the hour I first believed". As I type these lyrics, tears well up in my eyes. This could be called America's National Hymn. When sung in its soft tones, it resonates in almost every heart.

"Except For God's Grace," "He Giveth More Grace," "Gracious Spirit Holy Ghost," and "Grace That Is Greater Than Our Sin," "By Gracious Powers," "Ye Know That the Lord is Gracious," "The Lord is Gracious and Compassionate" are a few of the more well-known Hymns about grace. Scanning Hymnals, almost every song is about grace, even if the word itself is not mentioned. Modern worship songs are replete with grace, too numerous to adequately list.

Grace Abounding to the Chiefest of Sinners is a heartfelt tome from the imprisoned Christian John Bunyan from the 17th century. *Grace Awakening* by Chuck Swindoll, *All of Grace* by Spurgeon, *Grace* by Lucado, and *What's So Amazing About Grace?* by Yancey are a few of the more popular selections of Christian books about grace. *Grace To You* is one of the most popular Christian radio programs. Grace, God's grace, has intertwined itself deeply into our fabric. Possibly because we have all participated in God's grace.

The reason we exist is because of God's grace. God draws all men to Himself because of Calvary. Calvary, of course, is the ultimate example of grace. Omnipotent, Infinite, Holy God, humbles Himself in the form of a Servant, partakes of our humanity, dies a horrific, unjust death, becoming sin, just for us. All stand in need of God's grace, for all have sinned. This is the horror of Phariseeism, or moral superiority. Though one may be morally superior to another, the standard is not someone else, it is God. And all our righteousness' are filthy rags in His sight. We were all condemned to die. All of us. All of us have sinned. We deserve an eternity in the lake of fire, the second death. But grace, with arms stretched wide, calling whosoever will, enduring the cross, despising the shame, lingered between Heaven and earth, as God's Mediator, for you and for me. Grace resonates, because we have all experienced it, we all need it. Grace to you. It's not what you think, possibly. It's not the ability to sin and still make

Heaven. It's God's gracious plan for Heaven, that only God's grace could devise. Won't you partake of His love and grace today? Heaven is waiting to rejoice.

Other Books by Steven Waldron

Commentary On Genesis Volume 1
Discussions In Scripture Series
A Creationist Commentary

Commentary On Genesis Volume 2
Discussions In Scripture Series
A Creationist Commentary

Commentary On Genesis Volume 3
Discussions In Scripture Series
A Creationist Commentary

Is Unconditional Security Scriptural?

www.ingramcontent.com/pod-product-compliance
Lightning Source LLC
Chambersburg PA
CBHW030203100526
44592CB00009B/417